POETIC DELUSIONS

Emotions of Thought

Book 2

Paul Morabito

STAR INVESTMENT STRATEGIES LLC

ISBN: **1502414287**
ISBN-13: **978-1502414281**

DEDICATION

    This book is dedicated to the unheard creative minds of the time and master poets of the past that paved the way. Though poetry is a hard genre to survive in, it is the most descriptive, expressive, and heart-felt genre ever put on paper. These words before you I write for the craft and joy of it. No longer held by boundaries, rules, or the bottom line. These are the mindless ramblings of an American Dreamer. With words, all dreams come to life.

"Doing something once can get addicting. Doing it twice is admitting it." –Paul Morabito

CONTENTS

Acknowledgments

1   Love Flame

2   The Commoner

3   The Next Hand

4   Gypsy Spell

5   Kings and Masters

6   Precious Little Things

7   The Contract

8   Cloudy Rainbow

9   Please Help

10   Wish You Knew

11   Poetic Delusion

12   Damn Thee

13   Sitting Still

14   Peaceful Lake

15   Free Flight

16   Waves of Love

17   Trapped

18   Wish

19   Joyous Love

20. Born for Greatness

21. True Self

22. I Am

23. Last Dance

ACKNOWLEDGMENTS

I would like to thank God once again for helping me complete another project in such a short amount of time. I would also like to thank my loved ones for their support with my writing career. I hope my work can touch others and inspire or bring back precious memories of old or create motivation of thought.

1 LOVE FLAME

Red like fire.
It burns me inside.
Every time I draw near.
Her locks flow eternal.
Pouring with uncontainable love.
Effortless.
Touching my soul.
Exuding desire.
One with the wind.
Hiding mysterious playful eyes.
That can't be denied.
I dare not touch.
Perfection.
But endlessly admire.
The red fire.

That burns me to no end.
Every time I sense fear.
Her lock's brush comforts dear.
Soaring with uncontainable emotion.
Carefree.
Warming my chills.
Spilling tenderness.

One with my thoughts.
Blanketing all worthlessness from existence.
I dare not question.
Willingly.
And always endlessly admire.
The scorching love.
Of my red fire.

2 THE COMMONER

If I was but air.
I would surround her pale fair skin.
If a gambler was.
Her heart would still no chance win.
For what chance does a mere Pauper have?
To win the love of a maiden so graceful.

If I were only her beau.
I would be worn as bows do.
To be only noticed or glanced at.
Is to have won my prize.
Attained my story to all heirs tell.

Oh what poor man's fate.
To be born into peasantry.
Stripped of worthless clothes.
And all life's pleasantries.

All my gold.
For one moment's glance would give.
To have her starlet eyes.
Gaze upon a simpleton.

3 THE NEXT HAND

Which way the wind blows?
My mind is lost but Heaven knows.
Every day I look to scramble.
Words so far away yet still ramble.
Reaching for the next phrase.
Hoping for answers to free the daze.
This state can no longer endure.
Flesh and blood from heart I pour.
Spilled across the paper of life.
Abandoned by all and wife.
To live alone is fate and destiny.
Though I try so hard to win hand dealt to me.
Hoping for a reshuffle.
I play the next hand.

4 GYPSY SPELL

My eyes can't see.
The wicked sprawls of wizardry.
Thou has cast upon me.
To lose my way.

My nose can smell.
The evil you tell.
For others to secretly ring the bell.
Of rumors that aren't true.

What magic cast upon deaf ears?
To muster the men to raise their spears.
Your evil once again appears.
To haunt my dreams.

What false treacherous lips?
Scorn me by leather whips.
Vinegar to quench my sips.
What poison has been bestowed?

Body touched.
By devil's hand much.
Of what I won't have such.
My soul forever shines.
Protected divine.

5 KINGS AND MASTERS

Ever since the beginning of time.
Man has been ruled by other men.
Each nobler than the other.
Armies were built.
People destroyed.
For what?

Living your life in a world that should not be.
Open your eyes why the hell can't you see.
Might take from them but can't take nothing from me.
You don't know.
Who they are.
What it is.
They are the kings.
The kings.
The kings of pain.

Upon this day the world will change.
If not for all for me.
To achieve and win is so sweet.
Taste of total victory.
Upon this bloody field of death.
Across the lands from east to west.

Future lives we will save.
The short term cost for life is death.
To assure a fruitful future.
These wounds of war will far surpass the skills of simple suture.
But for blood to stop.
It must now ever flow.
So raise your hearts and souls with swords.
And off to death we go.

6 PRECIOUS LITTLE THINGS

A little leap.
Goes a long way.
A little faith.
Gets you through the day.
A little poem.
With thoughts of dismay.
Makes little life problems.
All go away.

A little love.
Can turn to bigger things.
A little praise.
Confidence of self brings.
A little kiss.
Which can't easily dismiss.
Makes little life problems.
Turn to joyful bliss.

A big raise.
Can't the reaper pay.
A big praise.
Selfish motive say.
A big burden.
Too heavy to weigh.

The big life.
Turning to decay.
Makes big life problems.
In thoughts stay.

It's the little things we should rejoice.
Not big issues without choice.
Those things we cannot change.
Should be left to ponder out mind's range.

7 THE CONTRACT

All I've gained.
All I lost.
Evil deals.
Come great cost.

Nothing earned comes easy.
Nothing learned comes cheap.
Evil deeds.
Wicked men souls do keep.

I was once good.
Now misunderstood.
Evil deals.
Destroyed brotherhood.

I had it all.
When I had none.
Evil deeds.
Took my sun.

Now I wait.
Eternal fate.
Bloody contract.
Signed with date.
I wish things were.

As before.
When all alone.
And stinky poor.

8 CLOUDY RAINBOW

My heart is painted.
The color red.
Reminds me of words.
You once said.

My tears are running.
The color blue.
Reminds me of things.
You used to do.

My sadness grows.
The color black.
For words I said.
I can't take back.

My memory fades.
The color green.
Wish I never forgot.
The fun we seen.

My days remorse.
The color yellow.
Never again.
To greet you hello.

My thoughts wonder.
The color brown.
What it would be.
To not once frown.

My eyes not blessed.
The color gold.
To share our laughter.
Wrinkly old.

My joy is stained.
The color gray.
Never again.
To love that way.

Your pictures framed.
The color badge.
I'm getting old.
While you don't age.

My days are numbered.
The colors of a cloudy rainbow.
Years lost spent.
Wishing it were me to go.

9 PLEASE HELP

My hand out and open.
Hoping for a token.
Of kindness loving gesture.
From strangers that pass.

Chilled to the bone.
As food cart my throne.
Displays my misfortune.
Welcome my home.

Filthy ground stricken.
Most think I'm tricking.
As cold eyes ignored.
The once loved son adored.

Pleading for pity.
From hunger rich city.
Heartless and annoyed.
People that destroyed.
My rights as human.

Though bruised and battered.
And all life's dreams shattered.
I hold my chin high.
Last looks at the sky.

Still wondering why.
You all let me die.

10 WISH YOU KNEW

From start to finish.
The race is won.
Through sad and precious moments.
Felt yesterday just begun.

Days flew by so quickly.
Was so long ago.
When I held you tightly.
Swore not to let go.

An angel's touch.
I sure do miss.
That sweet caress.
That farewell kiss.

Memories I foolishly gave way.
Now yearn for.
Each and every day.

Why torture myself?
I do not know.
Things I had.
Taken.
Or should've never let go.

Now I stare from afar.
My shiny bright star.
Not knowing my pain.
While driven insane.

The image of your face.
Tattooed in mind.
Walking aimlessly about.
Still seeking but can't find.

Though hurting and torn.
Those days never regret.
Most precious life's moments.
Were spent when we met.

Many miles and years.
Could not tears dry.
Each reminding look.
Of pictures staring at your eyes.

Shut out from your presence.
Can't even see or call.
Wishing I could tell you.
How I loved them all.

11 POETIC DELUSION

Forgive the poetic delusion.
Of my mind infiltrating with great intrusion.
Thoughts trapped in a box.
Must be cured and set free.
Unlocked.
For world to see.
Judgment comes.
Mind undone.
Creating poetry of music.
Art of words.
Unchained.
Nothing but alone.
The mind beckons and moans.
Waiting for a cure.
How much can one endure?
This typing.
Continuing on.
Will it even be read when gone?
What's the point?
Is there reason?
A purpose?
Confusion consumes.
The mind resumes.
To continue on.
Like an endless tick.

Here comes the tock.
Is this the joy?
I seek.
Is this my fate?
So bleak.
The notes play on.
Lead playing solo.
Lights go out.
To hide the inner self.
Hopes and dreams.
Put back on the shelf.
Waiting for the next chapter to begin.
Though longing for it all to end.
Until one hits the top.
Looking at mouths drop.
Until then the mind needs cured.
Disease free.
On paper.
The crowd roared.

12 DAMN THEE

Damsel be thee damned.
To steal my heart.
Though I love thee so.
It kills to be apart.
Is it better to have loved?
Better to have lost?
Now cursed to bear this cross?
How can one love again when one experienced tender genuinity?
How can one gaze upon another and find peace when one is blinded
by previous love's sincerity?
How can one touch the heart of another soul when your past caresses
have marked me eternal?
Damsel be thee damned.
To capture my every thought.
Imprisoned without appeal.
Caged behind mind's steel.
Ironic how I love my fate.
To be forever trapped.
In dreamful state.
Damsel be thee damned.
For loving me how you do.
Damsel be thee damned.
For me damning you.

13 SITTING STILL

Twas so long ago.
When all we had were smiles.
Holding hands.
Thought forever could walk miles.
Sitting in the gentle breeze.
Laughs and love came with ease.
Never a moment to be forced.
True love stayed the course.
Now I kneel upon the grass.
Lonely here though short time passed.
Name etched in hardened stone.
I still sit and wait alone.
Thinking of where I want to take her.
Forgetting still she met her maker.
All the years we had and spent.
Never tears since day we met.
Now puddles of emotion flow.
Alone still and can't let go.

14 PEACEFUL LAKE

Love at stake.
Upon peaceful lake.
Last day shared.
Love impaired.
My heart can't longer take.

You tremble and shake.
Upon tranquil lake.
First day loved.
Second time shoved.
Heart that's genuinely fake.

Took a while.
To learn your style.
See your true reflection.
Took a day.
To part away.
Cure this lethal injection.

Now you say it isn't true.
Oh my.
The things I'd do.
Upon peaceful lake.
To change your mind.

Wickedly entwine.
This trap forever more.

A poisoned kiss.
With murderous eyes.
A heart felt touch.
Filled with lies.
This is all I see.
Upon this peaceful lake.
If you had devil's power.
Surely souls you'd take.

I leave you now.
Forever.
To claim your next endeavor.
Alone upon this peaceful lake.
For I am free.
To always be.
The good man of honesty.
My true word defines me.

Gaze upon for the last.
Beneath peaceful waters.
I thee cast.
To drown the evil you amassed.
Upon this quiet tranquil lake.

15 FREE FLIGHT

Free bird fly.
High in sky.
Never die.
Angels don't cry.

Free bird fly.
High in sky.
Don't wonder why.
I left up high.

Free bird fly.
High in sky.
Don't waste lil tears.
Upon dry eyes.

Free bird fly.
High in sky.
Finally unchained.
From life sustained.

Bound bird free.
Never again see.
Pain and misery.

Others instilled in me.

Bound bird free.
Fell from tree.
Pushed unwillingly.
Tortured innocently.

Free bird fly.
High in sky.
Deserving loving justice grace.
Away from false hellish face.

Heavenly angel flew.
While gracious winds blew.
To opened golden skies.
Where no one ever lies.

16 WAVES OF LOVE

Riding the waves of love.
High tide crashing in from above.
No lifeguard can save.
This endless love that's you I crave.

Endless love.
Don't end this love. Yeah.
You're my number one.
Fastball fire caught in glove.

Casting out that line.
Hope to reel you in sometime.
All treasures from the deep.
Without you don't me complete. No.

Endless love.
Don't end this love. Yeah.
Reckless dove.
Wing clipped trying push and shove.
Stop.
It weighs a ton.
Please forgive for what I've done.

I'm just riding the wave of love.
Low tide thought would never come.

Now everyone can see.
What you really mean to me.
Because you're my number one.
So please don't ever say.
It's done.

17 TRAPPED

No matter what I do is wrong.
Every word hears another song.
Trapped in life's maze.
Never reaching the end.
Confused in mind's daze.
Never to comprehend.
The days that come and gone.
Here goes another song.
How does this tune end?
This constant reminder.
All life's work.
Fitting snug in just one binder.
Was it all worth it?
Will it be read and remembered?
Dead or dismembered?
All this time surrendered.
For you to casually read.
While author's hearts bleed.
Upon white screens of emptiness.

No matter what one writes is wrong.
For every word hears a song.
It's even worse to keep it in.
Mindful thoughts trapped is sin.
So here I go again.
Trapped between wrong or right.

Wishing to one day.
Be wrapped with love and in bright light.

18 WISH

I wish I could stop time.
Wish I could give the homeless my last dime.
Wish there was only peace.
Wish love would never cease.
Wish the losers finally won.
Wish for true love lost begun.
Wish the sick would get healed.
Wish for truth to be revealed.
Wish that loved ones never died.
Wish to never again spill tears I cried.
Wish to always do what's right.
Wish to lend the weak my might.
Wish the whole world would be saved.
Wish the wicked all behaved.
Wish the blind could see.
Wish my family loved me.
Wish for all eternal grace.
To splash upon my worthless face.

19 JOYOUS LOVE

Give the girls my love.
Showered with my touch above.
Always and forever more.
Two most things I adore.
I hold so close and dear.
To protect from doubt and remove fear.
Love is safe in daddy's arms.
Away from evil and all harms.
I give you both my last breath.
In life and even death.
All I have is yours.
Hope and love eternal pours.
All that matters is your love.
Your success is what my dreams are made of.
I wish my heart and knowledge teach.
To both be just and goals all reach.
For my happiness all depends.
On the means and the ends.
Of our joyous love.

20 BORN FOR GREATNESS

Every now and then great people are born.
These are the ones that touch the lives and hearts of many.
They are put here for a greater purpose.
To warm the world with love and sweetness.
To lend a helping hand when others turn away.
To willingly provide comfort and endearment to mourners in need.
To see and show others the vision of a peaceful world where children
of all races can love one another freely.
To discover the cure for individual suffering of the mind, heart, body,
and soul.
To feel compassion and sorrow for those who show none.
To openly love without question without expecting anything in return.
These are the rare few that make humankind great.
That make life worth living.
The true believers of hope for the future that pave the way for others
to follow.
The leaders of example.
The followers of wisdom and truth.
I was blessed and honored to be part of one of these rare individuals
lives that were born this day.
For I was just one of the many chosen they touched that made the
difference.
Be the difference in the world.
Show them your greatness.

21 TRUE SELF

Take the risk.
Upon moment's notice.
Never look back.
Do not retrace the past.
Take fresh steps towards new journeys.
Open doors of mystery.
Don't second guess the plan.
Stay the course.
Achieve success.
Set higher goals than feel attainable.
Reach for the stars.
Turn dreams into reality.
Feel the wind at your back.
Ride the wave of victory.
Inhale breaths of happiness.
Exude an aura of excellence.
Exhale all negativity.
Create art never seen before.
Love endlessly.
Build lifelong friendships.
Help others in need.
Teach the children the difference between right and wrong.
Lead the way.
Stand up when others wont or choose not to.
Be fearless when others cower.
Shine brightly in the darkness.

Show others the way when lost.
Don't be afraid to be different.
Use it to your advantage.
Garner strength from weakness.
Sacrifice pride.
Take on the burden of others that can no longer walk.
Be unselfish.
But most importantly.
Be yourself.

22 I AM

More than less.
But less than worthy.
Worthy to be heard.
But heard in silence.

Lesser than greater
But greater than those who think I'm less.
Lesser than perfect.
But perfect to the one that loves me.

Equal in creation.
But created to excel.
Excellent by design.
But designed to fail.

Added to the multitude.
But cast away in solitude.
All alone.
But never abandoned.

Subtracted and taken away.
But keep faith for another day.
Removed from the present picture.
But displayed for eternity.

Divided without option.

But optioned to not expire.
Expired by date.
But dated to live on.

Multiplied by happiness.
But rooted for stability.
Squared to build.
But built from flesh and blood.

23 LAST DANCE

The night is through.
Though wish it weren't.
To bid adieu.
I'll fight the current.

Time flew.
Though wish it stopped.
Till tomorrow's love concoct.

Body warm.
Though now cold.
Wish forever we'd grow old.

Whispered words in ear.
Though now windy and can't hear.
Your heart cries louder so.
Telling me not to go.

THE END

ABOUT THE AUTHOR

Paul Morabito is an American born fiction/nonfiction author raised in a close knit Italian-American family in the state of New Jersey. He had an amazing childhood until the sudden tragic death of his dear brother, Carmelo. It was this event that stirred the will and desire to succeed physically, mentally and artistically to make his brother and family proud. Paul took on and enjoyed martial arts where he excelled at a very young age. Determined to find another passion, Paul stumbled upon chess and another hidden musical talent which made him form a local band with childhood friends. He soon played lead guitar for many years to come as an accomplished musician. His love for music grew and still remains to this day as does his desire to release a solo album in the future.

On the path to achieving a degree in pharmacy, Paul discovered a great interest in English Literature where he focused on masterpiece tragedies and works such as those written by Shakespeare, Chaucer, and Poe. Little was known that this would spark a fire of inspiration to jump into the world of writing where creative minds blossom and run free. His career took over a decade long hiatus but was blessed with two beautiful princesses who are his everything. The urge to continue with his dream led to the release of three latest projects in the same year, stemming from an Evangelical Christian background. The author's faith in God remains strong and he entrusts his life, children and career in His hands. Paul plans to continue writing across all fictional genres and start filming his first cinematic production.

Website: Paul-Morabito.com

Made in the USA
Middletown, DE
27 March 2015